TROPICAL FISH H

Discover the vibrant world of Tropical

Fish: care, feeding, and Aquarium secrets

SANDRA D. SIMPSON

Table of Contents

CHAPTER ONE

INTRODUCTION TO

TROPICAL FISH

Tropical fish are a diverse group of fish species that thrive in warm, freshwater environments, typically found in regions near the equator. Their vibrant colors and unique behaviors make them a popular choice among aquarium enthusiasts. This introduction will delve into what tropical fish are, their history in the aquarium trade, and the benefits of keeping them as pets.

1.1 What Are Tropical Fish?

Tropical fish refer to a variety of fish species that inhabit warm waters, typically those found in regions between the Tropics of Cancer and Capricorn. These fish are generally adapted to thrive in temperatures ranging from 75°F to 80°F (24°C to 27°C) and can be found in various aquatic environments, including freshwater rivers, lakes, and coastal regions. The term "tropical fish" encompasses a wide range of species, including:

1. **Freshwater Tropical Fish:** These fish are found in rivers, lakes, and streams. Common examples include bettas, guppies, neon tetras, and angelfish. Freshwater tropical fish are often characterized by their vibrant colors and unique body shapes.

2. **Marine Tropical Fish:** While not the focus of this section, marine tropical fish inhabit the ocean's warmer waters. They include popular species like clownfish, tangs, and butterflyfish. Marine tropical fish typically require a saltwater environment, which poses different challenges for aquarists.

Tropical fish are often classified based on their behavior, size, and habitat preferences. Some species are peaceful and social, making them ideal for community tanks, while others may be more territorial and aggressive. Understanding the characteristics of various tropical fish is crucial for creating a harmonious aquarium environment.

1.2 History of Tropical Fish in Aquariums

The practice of keeping tropical fish in aquariums dates back several centuries. Here's a brief overview of the history and evolution of tropical fishkeeping:

1. **Early Beginnings:** The first known records of keeping fish in captivity date back to ancient Mesopotamia, around 5000 BCE. However, these early aquarists primarily kept fish for food and not for ornamental purposes.

2. **China's Influence:** In ancient China, around 2000 BCE, fish were kept in ponds and small

water containers for both aesthetic enjoyment and religious significance. Goldfish, a species originally bred from carp, became particularly popular and were among the first ornamental fish.

3. **19th Century Aquarium Development:** The modern aquarium began to take shape in the 19th century when the glass tank was invented. This innovation allowed fish enthusiasts to observe fish in a controlled environment. The establishment of public aquariums further fueled interest in tropical fish.

4. **Introduction of Tropical Species:** In the late 1800s, tropical fish were introduced to Europe from tropical regions, thanks to advancements in transportation and breeding techniques. The discovery of colorful species from South America, Africa, and Asia captured the imagination of aquarists and led to the widespread popularity of tropical fishkeeping.

5. **Advancements in Fish Care:** The 20th century saw significant advancements in aquarium technology, including filtration systems, heating devices, and improved water chemistry understanding. These developments made it easier for hobbyists to keep tropical fish healthy and thriving in their homes.

Today, tropical fishkeeping is a thriving hobby enjoyed by millions worldwide. Aquarists now have access to a wide array of resources, including books, online communities, and specialized stores, to help them maintain their aquatic environments.

1.3 Why Choose Tropical Fish?

Choosing tropical fish as pets offers numerous advantages, making them a favorite among aquarium enthusiasts. Here are several compelling reasons to consider:

1. **Diversity of Species:** The variety of tropical fish available is staggering, with thousands of species to choose from. Each species offers unique colors, patterns, and behaviors, allowing aquarists to create visually stunning aquascapes.

2. **Ease of Care:** Many tropical fish species are relatively easy to care for, making them suitable for beginners. With proper research and preparation, novice aquarists can successfully maintain healthy environments for their fish.

3. **Educational Experience:** Keeping tropical fish provides valuable learning opportunities about aquatic ecosystems, biology, and water chemistry. It fosters a sense of responsibility as aquarists monitor their fish's health and habitat.

4. **Stress Relief and Aesthetic Appeal:** Observing fish swimming in a well-maintained aquarium can be incredibly calming. The vibrant colors and movements of tropical fish add beauty to any space, making aquariums a popular choice for home and office decor.

5. **Community and Social Interaction:** The tropical fishkeeping community is vibrant and supportive. Joining local clubs or online forums allows enthusiasts to share experiences, trade fish, and exchange advice, fostering social interaction and friendships.

6. **Contribution to Conservation:** Many aquarists actively participate in conservation efforts, supporting sustainable fishkeeping practices and breeding programs for endangered species. By keeping tropical fish

responsibly, aquarists can help raise awareness about aquatic conservation.

In conclusion, tropical fish offer an exciting and rewarding hobby for individuals of all ages. Their stunning beauty, diverse species, and the joy of maintaining an aquarium create an enriching experience that captivates the hearts of fish enthusiasts worldwide. As we delve deeper into the world of tropical fish, we will explore various aspects, including care requirements, compatibility, and tips for creating thriving aquariums.

CHAPTER TWO
POPULAR TYPES OF
TROPICAL FISH

Tropical fish come in a vast array of species, each with its unique colors, patterns, and behaviors. Understanding the different types of tropical fish is essential for aquarists looking to create a thriving and visually appealing aquarium. In this section, we will explore the distinction between freshwater and saltwater tropical fish, highlight some iconic species, and provide guidance on choosing the right species for your aquarium.

2.1 Freshwater vs. Saltwater Tropical Fish

When it comes to tropical fishkeeping, the primary distinction lies between freshwater and saltwater species. Each type has its unique characteristics, care requirements, and challenges.

Freshwater Tropical Fish

Freshwater tropical fish inhabit rivers, lakes, and streams, thriving in environments where salinity levels are low. These fish are generally more accessible and cost-effective for aquarists. Some popular freshwater tropical fish include:

- **Guppies (Poecilia reticulata):** Known for their vibrant colors and playful behavior, guppies are hardy fish that breed easily in captivity. They are ideal for beginners and can thrive in community tanks.

- **Tetras (Family Characidae):** This group includes various species, such as neon tetras and cardinal tetras, recognized for their striking colors and small size. Tetras are peaceful schooling fish that thrive in groups, making them perfect for community aquariums.

- **Cichlids (Family Cichlidae):** Cichlids are a diverse group with numerous species, including angelfish, discus, and African cichlids. They can be more challenging to care for due to territorial behavior, but their stunning colors and personalities make them popular among aquarists.

- **Betta Fish (Betta splendens):** Betta fish are known for their flowing fins and vibrant colors. They are relatively easy to care for but can be aggressive, especially males, making careful selection of tankmates essential.

Saltwater Tropical Fish

Saltwater tropical fish inhabit ocean environments, where salinity levels are significantly higher than in freshwater. While they can be more challenging to maintain due to the complexity of saltwater aquariums, saltwater fish offer incredible beauty and diversity. Examples include:

- **Clownfish (Amphiprioninae):** Famous for their symbiotic relationship with anemones, clownfish are vibrant and easy to care for, making them a favorite for beginners venturing into saltwater aquariums.

- **Tang Fish (Family Acanthuridae):** Known for their vibrant colors and unique body shapes, tangs require larger tanks due to their active nature. Species like the blue tang are popular for their striking appearance.

- **Butterflyfish (Family Chaetodontidae):** Butterflyfish are known for their beautiful patterns and colors. While some species are hardy, others can be more sensitive to water quality, requiring experienced care.

- **Lionfish (Pterois):** Recognizable for their long, venomous spines and stunning appearance, lionfish can be kept in larger aquariums. However, they require careful handling and specific tank conditions.

2.2 Iconic Species: Guppies, Tetras, Angelfish, and More

Several species stand out as iconic representatives of tropical fishkeeping. These fish not only capture the attention of aquarists but also contribute significantly to the diversity and beauty of home aquariums. Here are a few noteworthy species:

1. Guppies (Poecilia reticulata):

Appearance: Guppies are small, brightly colored fish with males exhibiting a wide range of patterns and hues.

Behavior: They are social fish that thrive in groups and are known for their active nature. Guppies are also prolific breeders.

Care Requirements: They prefer a well-planted tank with stable water conditions and can tolerate a variety of water parameters, making them ideal for beginners.

2. Neon Tetras (Paracheirodon innesi):

- *Appearance:* Neon tetras are small, colorful fish characterized by their striking blue and red stripes.

- *Behavior:* These peaceful schooling fish should be kept in groups of six or more to thrive and feel secure.

- *Care Requirements:* They prefer slightly acidic to neutral pH levels and a well-planted tank with gentle filtration.

3. Angelfish (Pterophyllum scalare):

- *Appearance:* Angelfish are recognized for their unique triangular shape and elegant fins, often displaying stunning colors and patterns.

- *Behavior:* While generally peaceful, they can be territorial, especially during breeding. Proper tank mates should be chosen to avoid aggression.

- *Care Requirements:* They require a larger tank (at least 20 gallons) with stable water conditions and plenty of hiding spots.

4. **Discus (Symphysodon spp.):**

- *Appearance:* Discus are round, flat fish known for their vibrant colors and patterns, making them highly sought after by aquarists.

- *Behavior:* They prefer to be in small groups and can exhibit strong social behaviors.

- *Care Requirements:* Discus are sensitive to water conditions and require a well-maintained aquarium with specific temperature and pH levels.

5. Bettas (Betta splendens):

- *Appearance:* Betta fish are famous for their long fins and striking colors, ranging from vibrant reds and blues to more muted shades.

- *Behavior:* Males can be highly aggressive, particularly towards other males, while females are generally more tolerant. Careful selection of tank mates is essential.

- *Care Requirements:* Bettas can thrive in smaller tanks but benefit from a larger environment with plenty of hiding spots.

2.3 Choosing the Right Species for Your Aquarium

Selecting the right tropical fish for your aquarium is crucial for creating a harmonious and thriving environment. Here are several factors to consider when choosing species:

1. Tank Size:

- Different species have varying space requirements. Larger fish or more active species, such as cichlids, often need larger tanks, while smaller fish, like guppies or tetras, can thrive in smaller setups.

2. Water Parameters:

- Different species have specific water quality requirements, including temperature, pH, and hardness. Researching the needs of potential species is essential to ensure they can coexist in the same environment.

3. Compatibility:

- Consider the temperament and social behavior of the species you wish to keep. Some fish are more aggressive or territorial, which can lead to conflicts in a community tank. Grouping peaceful species together is often a successful strategy.

4. Breeding Behavior:

- If breeding is a consideration, be aware that some species, such as guppies and angelfish, may require specific conditions and tank setups for successful reproduction.

5. Maintenance Level:

- Some species are more demanding in terms of care than others. Beginners may want to start with hardy species like guppies or tetras before exploring more delicate options like discus or certain marine fish.

6. Aesthetic Preferences:

- The visual appeal of different species can influence your choices. Selecting fish that complement each other in color and form can enhance the overall beauty of your aquarium.

Overall, understanding the popular types of tropical fish, their distinctions, and the characteristics of iconic species is vital for anyone interested in creating a successful aquarium. By considering tank size, water parameters, compatibility, and personal preferences, aquarists can curate a stunning and harmonious aquatic environment that showcases the beauty of tropical fish. Whether you are a beginner or an experienced aquarist, the world of tropical fish offers endless opportunities for exploration and enjoyment.

CHAPTER THREE

SETTING UP THE PERFECT TROPICAL FISH AQUARIUM

Setting up a tropical fish aquarium is a rewarding endeavor that requires careful planning and consideration to create a thriving aquatic environment. From choosing the right size and shape of the aquarium to selecting the appropriate filtration, heating systems, substrates, and decorations, each element plays a crucial role in the health and well-being of the fish. This guide aims to provide an extensive and educational overview of the key factors involved in establishing the perfect tropical fish aquarium.

3.1 Aquarium Size and Shape

The size and shape of the aquarium are foundational aspects that significantly influence the success of your tropical fishkeeping experience. First and foremost, the size of the tank should be determined by the type and number of fish you plan to keep. A larger tank generally provides a more stable environment, as it can better absorb fluctuations in water quality and temperature. For beginner aquarists, a tank of at least 20 gallons is recommended, as it offers sufficient space for a variety of fish and facilitates easier maintenance. In contrast, smaller tanks can be more challenging to manage, particularly regarding water quality and temperature stability.

Additionally, the shape of the aquarium can impact the swimming patterns and behavior of the fish. Tall tanks are ideal for species that prefer vertical swimming spaces, such as angelfish, while longer, wider tanks are better suited for species that thrive in open water, like tetras and guppies. Moreover, the shape of the tank influences the distribution of light and the arrangement of decorations, which can create hiding spots and open swimming areas essential for the fish's comfort. Ultimately, selecting the right size and shape of the aquarium is a crucial first step in establishing a healthy environment for tropical fish.

3.2 Filtration and Heating Systems

Filtration and heating systems are critical components of a successful tropical fish aquarium, as they ensure a clean and stable environment for the fish. A good filtration system helps maintain water quality by removing waste products, uneaten food, and other debris. There are several types of filters available, including hang-on-back filters, canister filters, and sponge filters. Hang-on-back filters are popular among beginners due to their ease of installation and maintenance. Canister filters, on the other hand, provide superior filtration capabilities and are ideal for larger tanks or heavily stocked aquariums. It is important to choose a filter that is appropriately rated for the size of your tank and to perform regular maintenance, such as cleaning the filter media and replacing it as needed.

Heating systems are equally important, as most tropical fish require a stable water temperature between 75°F and 80°F (24°C to 27°C). An aquarium heater should be selected based on the tank's size and the specific temperature requirements of the fish species you plan to keep. Submersible heaters are the most common choice, as they can be easily adjusted and placed discreetly in the tank. To ensure accurate temperature readings, it is advisable to use a reliable aquarium thermometer. Monitoring water temperature regularly is essential, as fluctuations can stress fish and lead to health issues. Combining a good filtration system with a reliable heating system will create a healthy and stable environment that supports the well-being of your tropical fish.

3.3 Substrates and Decorations

Choosing the right substrates and decorations is essential for creating a visually appealing and functional tropical fish aquarium. The substrate serves as the foundation for the aquarium and can influence the overall aesthetic as well as the health of the fish. Common substrate options include gravel, sand, and specialized substrates designed for planted aquariums. Gravel is versatile and easy to clean, making it a popular choice for many freshwater aquariums. Sand, on the other hand, is ideal for species that prefer a softer bottom, such as certain types of catfish and loaches. When selecting a substrate, consider the needs of the fish you intend to keep and how the substrate will affect the overall look of the aquarium.

In addition to substrate, decorations play a vital role in providing hiding spots and enrichment for tropical fish. Live plants are highly beneficial as they offer natural hiding spaces, contribute to water quality by absorbing nitrates, and enhance the aquarium's aesthetic appeal. Artificial plants can also be used for decoration, although they do not provide the same environmental benefits as live plants. Other decorative elements, such as rocks, driftwood, and caves, can create a diverse landscape that encourages natural behaviors in fish, such as hiding, exploring, and spawning. It is important to ensure that all decorations are safe for aquarium use and free of sharp edges that could harm the fish.

In conclusion, setting up the perfect tropical fish aquarium involves thoughtful consideration of various factors, including aquarium size and shape, filtration and heating systems, as well as substrates and decorations. By selecting an appropriate tank size, investing in reliable filtration and heating systems, and carefully choosing substrates and decorations, aquarists can create a beautiful and thriving aquatic environment that enhances the health and well-being of their tropical fish. Proper planning and attention to detail in these areas will ensure a successful and enjoyable fishkeeping experience for both novice and experienced aquarists.

CHAPTER FOUR

WATER CHEMISTRY AND MAINTENANCE

Maintaining optimal water chemistry is crucial for the health and longevity of tropical fish. Properly balanced water parameters not only support the fish's well-being but also promote a stable and thriving aquarium ecosystem. In this section, we will explore the essential elements of water chemistry, the importance of regular water changes and filtration, and how to test and maintain ideal water conditions to create the best possible environment for your tropical fish.

4.1 Understanding Water Parameters (pH, Hardness, Ammonia)

Understanding key water parameters is vital to the success of any tropical aquarium. The primary factors to monitor include pH, water hardness, and ammonia levels. pH measures the acidity or alkalinity of the water, and different fish species have specific pH requirements. For example, most tropical fish prefer a pH range of 6.5 to 7.5, though certain species may thrive in slightly more acidic or alkaline water. Water hardness, which refers to the concentration of dissolved minerals such as calcium and magnesium, also affects the health of the fish. Soft water (low hardness) is preferred by species like tetras and angelfish, while others, such as livebearers, do well in harder water. Lastly, ammonia is a toxic byproduct of fish waste and uneaten food that can accumulate in the tank if not properly managed. High levels of ammonia can lead to stress, illness, or even death in fish, making it essential to monitor and control through regular water testing and proper filtration.

4.2 Managing Water Changes and Filtration

Water changes are a fundamental aspect of aquarium maintenance, helping to remove excess waste, uneaten food, and toxins while replenishing essential minerals. Regular water changes, typically 20-25% every one to two weeks, are necessary to maintain water quality and keep fish healthy. During water changes, it is important to use dechlorinated water that matches the temperature and pH of the aquarium to avoid shocking the fish. In addition to water changes, a reliable filtration system plays a crucial role in managing water quality. Filters remove physical debris, break down harmful substances like ammonia and nitrites through biological filtration, and ensure proper oxygenation of the water.

Different types of filters, such as mechanical, chemical, and biological, can be combined to achieve optimal filtration, keeping the aquarium environment clean and balanced.

4.3 Testing and Maintaining Ideal Conditions

Regular water testing is key to maintaining ideal conditions in a tropical fish aquarium. Testing kits are available for measuring important water parameters, including pH, ammonia, nitrites, nitrates, and water hardness. By routinely testing the water, aquarists can quickly identify imbalances or harmful spikes in ammonia and nitrites, which can be lethal to fish if left unchecked. Based on the test results, appropriate adjustments can be made, such as performing a water change, adding conditioners, or adjusting filtration settings. Consistency in water conditions is essential, as rapid fluctuations in pH, temperature, or ammonia levels can stress fish and weaken their immune systems. By staying vigilant with testing and responding promptly to any changes, aquarists can create a stable, healthy environment where tropical fish can thrive.

In summary, water chemistry and maintenance are integral to the long-term success of a tropical fish aquarium. By understanding and monitoring water parameters, managing regular water changes and filtration, and testing the water consistently, aquarists can ensure a safe and stable habitat for their fish. Proper water care not only supports the health and well-being of the fish but also fosters a vibrant and balanced aquarium ecosystem.

CHAPTER FIVE

FEEDING TROPICAL FISH

Feeding tropical fish is a crucial aspect of aquarium care, as a well-balanced diet directly impacts the health, growth, and vitality of the fish. Tropical fish have diverse nutritional requirements based on their species, and providing the right types and amounts of food is key to maintaining a healthy aquarium environment. This section will explore the nutritional needs of different species, various types of fish food, and the importance of establishing a proper feeding schedule to ensure your tropical fish thrive.

5.1 Nutritional Needs of Different Species

Different species of tropical fish have varying nutritional needs, which must be met to ensure their overall health. Some fish, like guppies and mollies, are omnivorous, requiring a mix of plant-based and protein-rich foods. Herbivorous species, such as plecos and certain types of tetras, primarily consume algae and plant matter and benefit from foods high in fiber and plant-based nutrients. Carnivorous species, including bettas and angelfish, need a diet rich in proteins and fats, often derived from live or frozen prey. Additionally, the size and feeding habits of each species can influence their dietary needs; for instance, bottom-dwellers like catfish require sinking pellets, while mid-water swimmers prefer floating foods. Ensuring that the diet of each species mimics their natural food sources is crucial to maintaining their health, growth, and vibrant coloration.

5.2 Types of Fish Food (Pellets, Flakes, Frozen, Live)

Fish food comes in several forms, each serving different purposes and offering varying nutritional benefits. Flake food is one of the most common types, suitable for many surface-feeding species. It is convenient, easy to store, and provides a balanced diet for general fish populations. However, it can lose nutritional value quickly if not stored properly. Pellets, another common food type, are available in both sinking and floating varieties, catering to species that feed at different water levels. Pellets generally offer higher nutritional density than flakes and can be formulated for specific types of fish, such as carnivores or herbivores.

Frozen foods, such as bloodworms, brine shrimp, and daphnia, provide a more natural feeding experience and are rich in proteins and essential nutrients. These foods are ideal for supplementing the diet of carnivorous or omnivorous species. Live foods, like small invertebrates or larvae, offer the most natural feeding method and are excellent for species that hunt in the wild. However, live foods can carry the risk of introducing parasites or diseases, so it's essential to source them from reliable suppliers. A varied diet, combining flakes or pellets with frozen or live food, ensures that tropical fish receive the full spectrum of nutrients they need.

5.3 Feeding Schedules and Tips for Healthy Fish

Establishing a proper feeding schedule is essential for maintaining the health and well-being of tropical fish. Overfeeding is one of the most common mistakes in fishkeeping and can lead to poor water quality, as uneaten food decomposes and raises ammonia levels. Most tropical fish should be fed small amounts of food once or twice a day, ensuring they consume all the food within a few minutes. It is better to underfeed than overfeed, as fish can always be fed more if needed, but overfeeding can have serious consequences for both the fish and the aquarium environment. For some species, occasional fasting days or reduced feeding can promote healthy digestion and prevent issues like bloating.

Observing the behavior of your fish during feeding times is also important. Healthy fish will be active and eager to eat. If fish appear lethargic or disinterested in food, it could indicate illness or stress. Additionally, varying the diet and feeding times can mimic natural conditions, providing mental stimulation for the fish. Using automatic feeders for consistency, especially when away from home, can help maintain a regular feeding routine. By following these feeding practices, aquarists can support the health and longevity of their tropical fish while maintaining a clean and balanced aquarium environment.

Overall, feeding tropical fish involves understanding the specific nutritional needs of different species, choosing the right types of food, and maintaining a proper feeding schedule. A varied and well-balanced diet, combined with mindful feeding practices, will ensure that your tropical fish remain healthy, active, and vibrant. Regular observation and adjustment of feeding habits will further enhance their overall well-being and the long-term success of your aquarium.

CHAPTER SIX

TROPICAL FISH HEALTH AND DISEASE PREVENTION

Tropical fish are beautiful, yet delicate creatures that require specific care to maintain their health. Proper knowledge of fish diseases and prevention strategies is essential for every aquarist to ensure a thriving aquarium environment.

6.1 Common Tropical Fish Diseases

Tropical fish are susceptible to a variety of diseases, often caused by poor water quality, stress, or infections. Some of the most common diseases include:

1. **Ich (White Spot Disease):** Ich is a parasitic infection causing white spots on the fish's body and fins. Fish often scratch against objects to relieve discomfort. The disease can spread rapidly if left untreated.

2. **Fin Rot:** This bacterial or fungal infection causes the fins to fray and deteriorate. Poor water quality and stress are common triggers for fin rot, and it can affect a fish's overall health.

3. **Velvet Disease:** A protozoan infection, velvet disease causes a golden, dust-like film on the fish's skin. It is often accompanied by rapid gill movement and lethargy.

4. **Fungal Infections:** Fungal infections manifest as cotton-like growths on the fish's body. They

often occur after injury or in fish with weakened immune systems.

5. **Swim Bladder Disease:** This condition affects the fish's ability to swim properly, causing them to float awkwardly or sink. It is often linked to overfeeding or constipation.

6.2 Recognizing Symptoms and Treatment Options

Early detection is critical in treating fish diseases and preventing the spread to other tank mates. Common symptoms to look out for include:

1. **Behavioral Changes:** Lethargy, loss of appetite, or erratic swimming are often early signs of illness. Fish that isolate themselves or breathe heavily may also be in distress.

2. **Physical Symptoms:** White spots, lesions, ragged fins, bloated bellies, or discoloration are key indicators of specific infections. Bulging

eyes (pop-eye) or swollen bodies can suggest internal bacterial infections.

3. **Treatment Options:**

- **Ich Treatment:** Ich can be treated by raising the water temperature gradually and using medications such as copper-based treatments or malachite green.

- **Fin Rot Treatment:** Improving water quality and using antibacterial or antifungal treatments can reverse fin rot in its early stages.

- **Velvet Disease Treatment:** Copper-based medications and dimming the aquarium lights can help eliminate the protozoa causing velvet disease.

- **Fungal Infection Treatment:** Medications like antifungal fish dips and aquarium salt are effective in treating fungal growths.

- **Swim Bladder Disease Treatment:** Reducing feeding, offering high-fiber foods like peas, and maintaining stable water parameters can help manage swim bladder issues.

6.3 Preventing Illness Through Proper Care

Prevention is always better than cure when it comes to tropical fish health. A few key practices can help reduce the risk of diseases:

1. **Maintain Water Quality:** Regular water changes, appropriate filtration, and monitoring water parameters (pH, temperature, ammonia, nitrate, and nitrite levels) are vital for a healthy environment. A clean, stable environment minimizes stress and boosts the immune system of fish.

2. **Avoid Overcrowding:** Overcrowded tanks increase stress and make fish more vulnerable

to diseases. Follow species-specific recommendations for the number of fish per gallon.

3. **Quarantine New Fish:** New fish should be quarantined for at least two weeks before being introduced into the main tank. This prevents the spread of diseases that new fish might carry.

4. **Provide a Balanced Diet:** A varied, high-quality diet strengthens a fish's immune system. Avoid overfeeding, as leftover food can pollute the water and lead to bacterial growth.

5. **Observe Regularly:** Regularly observe your fish for any signs of distress or illness. Early detection allows for prompt treatment, reducing the risk of an outbreak.

By understanding common tropical fish diseases, recognizing symptoms, and maintaining proper care, you can ensure that your aquarium remains a healthy and vibrant environment for your fish.

CHAPTER SEVEN

BREEDING TROPICAL FISH

Breeding tropical fish can be a rewarding and fascinating endeavor for aquarium enthusiasts. However, successful breeding requires understanding the specific needs of different species and creating an environment conducive to reproduction. This section will explore the ideal breeding conditions for popular species, techniques to encourage breeding behavior, and best practices for caring for fry and raising healthy fish.

7.1 Ideal Breeding Conditions for Popular Species

The breeding requirements of tropical fish vary widely depending on the species, and creating the right environment is crucial for successful reproduction. For livebearers like guppies, mollies, and swordtails, breeding tends to occur naturally in community tanks, as these species do not require specific conditions to reproduce. However, to improve breeding success, providing dense plant cover or breeding traps can protect newborn fry from being eaten by adult fish. In contrast, egg-laying species like tetras, angelfish, and cichlids require more specific conditions. For example, angelfish need a flat surface, such as a leaf or breeding cone, to lay their eggs, while cichlids often prefer caves or secluded spaces. Maintaining optimal water parameters, including stable temperature and pH, is essential for many species, with slight adjustments in temperature often triggering spawning. Additionally, ensuring low stress levels by avoiding overcrowding and providing proper filtration contributes to creating a favorable breeding environment.

7.2 How to Encourage Breeding Behavior

Encouraging breeding behavior in tropical fish often involves recreating conditions that closely mimic their natural habitats. Many species respond to environmental changes, such as a slight increase in water temperature or changes in lighting cycles, which signal the onset of their breeding season. For instance, raising the temperature by a few degrees can stimulate spawning in fish like tetras and angelfish. Similarly, providing high-quality, protein-rich food such as live or frozen daphnia or bloodworms can enhance the fish's condition and prompt breeding behavior. Another effective technique is simulating seasonal changes, such as increasing water flow or performing partial water changes with cooler water, which can mimic rainfalls in the wild and encourage fish to spawn. For territorial species like cichlids, offering secluded spaces or visual barriers in the tank can create a sense of security, promoting courtship and mating.

7.3 Caring for Fry and Raising Healthy Fish

Once breeding has occurred, special care must be taken to ensure the survival and growth of the fry (baby fish). In livebearer species, fry are born fully developed and need immediate access to hiding places, such as dense plants or breeding boxes, to protect them from being eaten by adult fish. In contrast, egg-laying species produce eggs that need to be safeguarded until they hatch. Some fish, like angelfish and discus, exhibit parental care by guarding their eggs and fry, but in many cases, removing the eggs or fry to a separate breeding tank is necessary to ensure their survival.

Feeding is a critical aspect of raising healthy fry. Newly hatched fry require very fine food, such as infusoria, baby brine shrimp, or specially formulated fry food, depending on the species. It is important to feed them small amounts multiple times a day, as they grow rapidly and need constant nourishment. As they mature, they can gradually be introduced to crushed flakes or pellets. Keeping the water clean is essential during this stage, as fry are more sensitive to poor water conditions. Regular water changes and proper filtration, along with maintaining stable water parameters, will support their healthy development. Monitoring their growth and ensuring they have ample space to swim and develop will result in strong, vibrant fish that can eventually be integrated into the main aquarium.

CHAPTER EIGHT
TROPICAL FISH TANK MAINTENANCE AND LONG-TERM CARE

Maintaining a tropical fish tank involves a commitment to regular upkeep and proper care to ensure a healthy and balanced environment for your fish. A well-maintained aquarium can provide a thriving ecosystem that promotes the health and longevity of its inhabitants. This section explores the essential tasks involved in routine maintenance, effective cleaning and algae control methods, and best practices for long-term care to enhance the lifespan of tropical fish.

8.1 Routine Maintenance Tasks

Routine maintenance is crucial for keeping a tropical fish tank in optimal condition. It involves several tasks that help maintain water quality, control waste buildup, and ensure the well-being of the fish. One of the most important aspects of maintenance is performing **regular water changes**. Typically, replacing 10-20% of the tank's water every week helps dilute harmful substances such as ammonia, nitrites, and nitrates, which can accumulate and become toxic over time. This practice also replenishes essential minerals that fish need for health and vitality.

Another critical task is **monitoring water parameters**, including temperature, pH, ammonia, nitrite, and nitrate levels. These factors can fluctuate due to factors like waste accumulation, fish metabolism, or the introduction of new plants or fish. Regular testing, using test kits, ensures that the water remains within safe ranges, preventing stress or illness in the fish.

Filter maintenance is also essential to keep the tank's filtration system functioning efficiently. Filters collect debris, leftover food, and waste, and if left uncleaned, they can become clogged, reducing their effectiveness. Depending on the type of filter, cleaning or replacing filter media (sponges, cartridges, or bio-media) on a monthly basis is typically necessary. However, care should be taken not to clean all filter media at once, as this can remove beneficial bacteria needed for biological filtration.

8.2 Cleaning and Algae Control

Cleaning a tropical fish tank goes beyond water changes and filter maintenance. It also involves removing debris, preventing algae growth, and keeping the tank visually appealing. One of the most common issues in fish tanks is **algae buildup**, which, if left unchecked, can overgrow and reduce the tank's aesthetic appeal while depleting oxygen levels at night. Regular cleaning of the tank's surfaces with an algae scraper or magnetic cleaner helps keep algae under control.

Algae can accumulate on the glass, decorations, plants, and even the substrate, so addressing it regularly is necessary.

Introducing **algae-eating species**, such as certain catfish (like plecos) or snails, can help naturally control algae. These species consume different types of algae and contribute to keeping the tank cleaner. However, they should not be relied upon as the sole method of algae control.

Gravel vacuuming is another important cleaning task. Food particles, fish waste, and other debris settle on the tank floor and can contribute to poor water quality if not removed. Using a gravel vacuum during water changes ensures that the substrate stays clean and prevents harmful bacteria from building up. Additionally, any decorations, plants, or rocks should be periodically cleaned to remove algae or debris buildup. Care should be taken not to use harsh chemicals during cleaning, as these can be toxic to fish; simple scrubbing with water or specialized aquarium-safe tools is sufficient.

8.3 Long-Term Care and Enhancing Fish Lifespan

Long-term care is essential for ensuring the well-being and longevity of tropical fish. One of the most critical aspects of long-term care is **maintaining stable water conditions** over time. Fish are highly sensitive to changes in their environment, and fluctuations in temperature, pH, or water chemistry can cause stress and lead to illness. It's essential to maintain a consistent water temperature appropriate for the species being kept, usually between 75°F and 80°F (24°C to 27°C) for most tropical fish, with stable pH levels that suit their needs.

Another key to enhancing the lifespan of tropical fish is providing a **balanced diet**. Over time, feeding your fish a variety of high-quality foods, including flakes, pellets, frozen or live foods, helps ensure they receive the nutrients needed for optimal health. Avoiding overfeeding is also important, as uneaten food can rot and degrade water quality, contributing to an unhealthy environment. Many species benefit from occasional fasting or feeding smaller portions to mimic their natural feeding habits and prevent obesity-related issues.

Observation is also critical for long-term care. Regularly observing fish behavior allows early detection of any issues. Fish that are swimming erratically, showing signs of stress, or have changes in coloration or appetite may be experiencing health problems. Catching these signs early makes it easier to take corrective action, whether by adjusting water conditions or seeking treatment for disease.

Finally, **creating a stress-free environment** through proper tank setup, adequate space, and hiding spots can significantly improve fish health and longevity. Overcrowded tanks can lead to aggression, stress, and increased waste buildup, all of which can shorten a fish's life. Ensuring that fish are compatible in terms of temperament and tank size is vital for maintaining harmony in the aquarium. Regular maintenance, clean water, a stable environment, and a stress-free space will all contribute to the long-term well-being of tropical fish, helping them live full, healthy lives.

In conclusion, maintaining a tropical fish tank requires a combination of routine tasks, effective cleaning strategies, and thoughtful long-term care practices. By following these principles, aquarists can create a stable, healthy environment where tropical fish can thrive for years to come.

CONCLUSION

In conclusion, keeping tropical fish offers a unique and rewarding opportunity to create and maintain a vibrant, aquatic ecosystem in your home. With the right knowledge and dedication to aquarium setup, water chemistry, feeding, and routine care, you can ensure the health and well-being of these colorful species. From selecting the right fish and equipment to understanding their specific needs, a successful tropical fish tank requires attention to detail and ongoing maintenance. By providing a balanced, stable environment, you can enjoy the beauty and tranquility of tropical fish while fostering a long-lasting, thriving habitat.

Printed in Great Britain
by Amazon

54945372R00035